AF426622

EAT PASTA, RUN FASTA!

by Christopher George

Copyright © 2023 by Christopher George

All rights reserved.

ISBN 979-8218291945

No portion of this book may be reproduced in any form without written permission from the publisher or author, except as permitted by U.S. copyright law.

Eat pasta, run fasta

Drink water, less hotter

Have salmon, keep jammin'

Eat prawns,
grow strong

A little cheese, if you please

It takes two to tango...
...or split a mango

Have some yogurt
so your tummy
don't hurt

A little spinach
for a fast pitch

Local heroes eat
lots of gyros

Lots of
generals eat
their lentils

Even scholars
like a little
peach cobbler

A long day of mergers calls
for a burger

A balanced breakfast is a must, so plan ahead or you'll be late for the bus!

If you go skiing and it gets too icy, have some chili that's warm & spicy

A silly goose was on the loose,
riled up on lots of juice

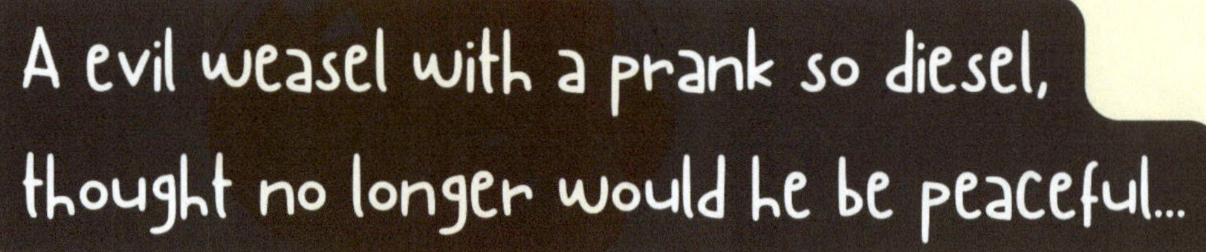

A evil weasel with a prank so diesel,
thought no longer would he be peaceful...
...later a bellow, "that cheeky fellow!
He filled my cello with yellow jell-o!"

My dad boasts for beans on toast, but when
I pull his finger...the smell sure does linger

The court took a recess, it wasn't unlawful, to put aside differences, and order falafel

Grandpa loves his hot fried chicken, says it keeps him alive and kickin'

Grandma's garden was sometimes smelly...
...she said it was the secret to her tasty jelly

Uncle Jean was never mean,
liked to farm his leafy greens

In the summer,
Cousin Louie
always cooked
his Ratatouille.
It was colorful, fresh,
and very healthy.
It was as tasty
as it was gooey.

My sister Tonya loves lasagna,
but not great news for her white pajamas

I was sad when my goldfish died, he was buried in the garden, to keep him nearby. But in the summer, I knew his spirit survived, cus above him grew tomatoes, and boy, did they thrive!

Some kids have allergies
and that's ok,
because they're all special
in every way.

The grown-ups argue about what foods are better, but always agree it tastes better together.

When life gives you lemons, make lemonade.

Enjoy and take pride in what you have made.

Eat pasta, run fasta,
and give thanks
every day.

For my beloved new family, friends, and neighbors, with whom we break bread. May we always share with those in need and sustain the bounty of the Earth for future generations.

-C.G.

www.ingramcontent.com/pod-product-compliance
Lightning Source LLC
Chambersburg PA
CBHW042116110726
48006CB00002B/653